Roses & Rain:
A Volume Of Poetry ❧

I hope you enjoy!

Tunnels of Laughter...

Great celebrations bring smiles & good thought.
Annual punctuations give reason.
Sounds excite youth in love with the season
While parents barely budget what was bought.

Tunnels of laughter & screams in the air
From children running around all about
Bring bliss & this hardly leaves room for doubt
In our minds that the future demands care &

A New Way…

Why even utter with no intent 2 mean?
Supply your opportunities with content.
Prison walls surround instead of a nice scene
For empty words lacking what one truly meant.

Time lapses slowly perceived by the victim.
Outside motion may be missed everyday
But think about our universal system
& soon u will begin 2 start a new way.

Lava...

She cracks the door open.
He looks in the mirror.
She blows a kiss at him
With lava in her heart.

No words need be spoken.
Bodies become nearer.
The light alters 2 dim
& they aren't pulled apart ❤

Crystal Eyes...

Moments may disappear soon.
O the time! Where did it go?
Oceans still reach for the moon
Despite them being so low.

Capture what u want of me.
Keep me in mind when I'm gone.
Rituals for memory
Help note when we were alone.

Life Without Love...

What is my life if you're not having one with me
& If I'm not having one with u?
What is this life without love?
What is this life without love?

What is our life if we are bound & are not free?
Here, read my heart if u want 2,
For what is this life without love?
What is this life without love?

Victor Without A Gun...

Some have memories devoid of sunshine.
Yearns 2 be next 2 a soul that's benign
May bring a depression intensively
Because darkness hides what we want 2 see.

Recall that u didn't create the sun
& u can be victor without a gun!
That which u crave may be hid within u
& rapidly grows when sunbeams glow thru ☀

Evil Confessions...

One wonders love this much & love felt in Heaven.
One seeks wisdom in why days of a week are seven.

I guess my love for u is far incomplete my darling.
Sweetheart, let's shed our past like a starling.

Join this world for a time & learn lovely lessons.
We keep all secrets & have no evil confessions 🍎

Moon Gossip...

In the essence of our hearts,
Adventures are desired.
Lapis Lazuli & Quartz aid the travel.
Informative missions can help those living
With anxiety struggles that attack their feelings.

It's awesome when love imparts
Conciseness that's required.
Its views extend beyond stars & earth gravel.
Strive & in the end, be amongst the giving
For special results in this temporal life's dealings ❦

Hyena Skin...

African rituals may uncover pathways
That lead 2 protection without any fault.
Hyenas stare with convincing eyes
At Sufis who are awake inside.
Moons brighten nights as well as days
& signal when activities halt.
Beasts such as these know the value of cries,
For groups appear when their sounds betide.
The skin of hyenas may carry a secret.
Sufis work strangely 2 most mortals.
Demons & witches try hard 2 beset
These two but they seem 2 escape thru portals.
Africa has many stories 2 tell
& I'm eager 2 make her feel well ❦

Cosmic Pirates...

They watch from a distance, seeking a chance
2 interrupt frequencies in the mind.
Their Psychic Martial Arts make sure a trance
Bewitches so that they'll have an entrance
Into a host they'll aggressively bind.

Cosmic Pirates have been here long before
Kings decided 2 take over the world.
A global craving at his very core
Is manipulated by those who soar
After insults toward his kingdom are hurled.

When bodies are taken over by force,
Warnings were spurned by arrogant beings.
This brings about something else from the source
Like maimed bloodlines that remain on a course
That leads them 2 awful pain for eons.

Crystals seem 2 capture ancient essence.
Those who understand are useful today.
The nature of stones may hide senescence
(Even in users for many crescents)
While blocking attacks that may come their way.

Prayers also help eliminate pain
Inflicted by these hard 2 see experts.
Those overtaken may appear insane
Like fast drivers who refuse their own lane
& misuse signals for safety alerts.

There are smokes that one can use 2 repel
Useless presence & unwanted luck.
Take from the fragrance & return the smell.
Unlock your chamber that helps u see well.
U may avoid traps where many get stuck.

There are other ways 2 guard your treasure
But unlike humans, these watchers aren't flesh.
They seem 2 know if one cheats for pleasure
(Leaving themselves open beyond measure)
Only 2 be robbed of form by their mesh.

After U Fell...

How dare anybody attack those who cared?
Pure meditation helps broken hearts get well.
Tranquility soon surrounds those impaired
When they remain calm even if they are scared.

Trust can be used 2 escort out of a shell
But never advertise secrets if they're shared.
Deceitful people will pretend you're wayward
Enough 2 have a lie that u want 2 tell,

As if u never got up after u fell ❦

A Lovely Question...

If lovely is the answer 2 the question,
We wouldn't have had 2 change who we
Were 2 end the corruption.
Together, we can do it. U & I with love but
How will true love come?
Will u be yourself & love someone?
Life can be so much better for u..
Be truthful, don't u think so too?
2 see my message, read the first word in every line.
U will have a message 2 find ❤

Imagine –

Claira...

I was speaking with one in the French Riviera,
Emotionally & her name was Claira.
She's found in dreams & some call her Temptation.
Her symbols reveal detailed information.
She colors her station
With shades of lavender
& once the elation,
I wished I could grab her.
She can be confusing but I understand
That sometimes, things don't go as planned.
Her eyes showed love & curiosity
As I woke devoid of animosity.
I was speaking with one in the French Riviera.
I'm not even sure if her name is Claira.

Mixed Evidence...

It slips like oil.
It's smooth as satin.
Its bold & royal
Like Roman Latin ✹

Dainty Candor...

It's amazing now,
A pure wondrous thing!
It's over my brow.
It's beyond my wing.
I don't understand.
I may never know.
I'll offer my hand
If it helps u grow.
What defines beauty
Save love lest it's true?
Exceptionally,
I find it with u ✿

Image Help...

If u see one, don't become too alarmed.
She wants 2 be assured that she's not harmed.

Suddenly, the locked doors open inside.
What one used 2 bury, now will not hide.

Imaginations manipulate growth.
Life & freedom made some people want both.

Gifts from another side of a mirror
May include crystals that make things clearer.

Happiness...

Honey & coconuts
& litanies of laughter
With nice Peridot cuts
Scream get what you're after!

Organic Opulence...

Some want the entire Earth
While others want an ocean
& what we need is self-worth
Before access will open.

We may plan ahead for riches 2 come
But snakes may poison support with deceit.
Remember the substance whence u come from.
Decisions impact what's under your feet 🍎

Green Neurosis...

My feelings for u are mutual
& I confess that your love is beautiful.

I revolve around its eloquence
As moons & I ponder the relevance.

I become anxious when I hear your name
But discover the person not 2 be the same

So I continue 2 feel neurotic.
I never knew love was so hypnotic.

Ramadan Moon...

The moon in Ramadan is so bright!
Kiss your family & have a good night.
Walk 2 the rug & pray al-witr..
Relax in peace while making zikr ❧

Struggle For Better...

Some try 2 avoid the inevitable
But prophecy spoken says otherwise.
2 trounce oppression is pleasurable.
We halt before speaking 2 escape lies.

Missions require strong women & men.
Enemies retreat due 2 influence.
We ask Allah for forgiveness of sin
& watch victories unfold with these blueprints ✺

Days of Shawwal...

The days of Shawwal are sweet & splendid!
Enjoy fruit, for Ramadan has ended
But don't be fooled by the loosed.
Keep your nafs in a noose
& eyes on a prize worth efforts induced.
Stay up for the challenge!

The Reward is great!

Scarlet Scarves...

Violets are violet & Roses are rose.
Views seen by a pilot lifts what he knows.
Big scarlet scarves can be your crystal's place
& used as portals for walking thru space ✪

Light House...

Crystals surround me.
The black ones ground me.
Green Moldavite lifts my inner-person
While my
Pistols are astounding! See?
"Brrraaaack" is the sound as we
Mean 2 hold 'em tight when rifts begin 2 worsen.

Signs Overhead...

Sun shine. Sun shine. Please show light!
Help us know everything will be all right.
Moon, light the night & make it bright.
These signs overhead expand insight ✿

Keep Traveling...

Worlds may collide but remain dedicated.
Sites where ships glide may seem evaporated.
It's more 2 this life than what meets naked eyes
& never forget the value of your cries ✿

Bad Drugs...

Please stay away from awfully bad drugs!
Our bodies should matter much more 2 us.
Concentrate on giving family hugs
Or ride away with police in a bus.

Your mind is precious & u can not see
If dangerous spots inside u increase.
Youth follow the standards we set freely
So let us do more good so crime can cease.

Clarity...

Grab the importance.
Let the truth be told.
Strength grows more intense.
It's worth more than gold ✿

Karamaat...

A blessed student has a master teacher.
Proper lessons make them afraid of naught.
The prudent teacher makes life easier
& these are proofs that honor what was brought ✿

Saturday Blossoms...

Love your soul enough 2 pray.
Prepare for another day.
Bestow what lasts a long while.
Sometimes, it may be a smile ☺

Imagine –

Pearls & Mermaids...

Some sailors move far from the shore.
Enchanting, mystic waters roar.
Some asked the captain, "What's it for?"
He says, "O my friends! I need some more,
For theirs are best & you'll agree."
He means the pearls from deep in sea.
The treasures drape Her Majesty.
She seems 2 use them occultly ✿

Green Pod/Clear Portal (pt. 1)...

Ponder how failure consumes the mortal.
Raise your portal, for I won't conceal
As I place gold on an antique torsel
2 weigh the force of energy we feel.

Green Pod/Clear Portal (pt. 2)...

Inside a clear portal (aiming upward)
Is a liquid that helps u shift at will.
The outside world has none in their cupboard
But surely those briefed enjoy the green chill 🌿

Artistic Expressions...

A work of art transcends emotions.
Doors open & welcome traffic.
Roads lead 2 an amazing classic.
Unspeakable cheers cement devotions ❦

A Nice Place...

Come on my friend & go with me.
Grab your bags & we're on our way.
We'll find adventures plain 2 see
& our admission there is free.
It's a safe place for us 2 stay.

Perfumes surround the strong windows.
Pillows & rugs for prayers & talks
Help strengthen us & evade foes,
Converse with good innuendos
& give comfort even on walks 🍎

Romantic Amazing...

Roses & Rain
So beautifully mix.
As I watch thru my pane,
I feel my heart fix.
No worries will last
When rain kiss a rose.
Emotions come fast.
Gracefully, it grows ❧

Valiant Group...

When u all go away,
It seems this town lacks a lot.
With uneasy frail delight,
I now recall what I forgot.

Viewed in your absence, I can see.
My thoughts become more amplified.
I love your presence all the more
For reasons that can't be denied.

Though when u part, I trust Allah!
O grant them safety & treasure!
Protect the cargo as they travel.
Fill their hearts with great pleasure
(Amen)!

Learn, if just a small amount,
For me & those who stayed behind.
O Valiant Group! Cherish your stay
& share with me what u may find ❧

Imagine –

Voyage...

Beautiful language moves the soul.
Knights in armor hold keys 2 love.
Hearts feel power that can heat coal.
(She said) Pour your sweetness into my bowl
& feed our pinkish lavender dove.

Signs hypnotically open the doors.
Shinning light enters & takes us away.
Travel in water far away from shores.
Whales look curiously at the explorers.
Beasts in the ocean will do as we say.

Beasts in the ocean will do as we say ☺

Pillows & Bears...

As if the girl wanted 2 be special,
She didn't care about a lot of things.
As long as problems were not medical,
She thought she knew the joy of what fun brings.

She frequently questioned about her soul.
Her actions make her seem like she's in love.
Flesh was only used as a means 2 a goal.
Most men couldn't fathom what she dreams of ✿

Queens, Kings & Peasants...

The world is a mess
So I grab my pen.
Monsters may play Chess
But neither will win.
Some hinder & may
Handcuff an artist,
(Restricting today)
A move not smartest.
Carefully support.
Share in heart & brain.
Then u won't abort
But have more 2 gain ❧

Days & Nights...

Nice, beautiful day!
Great, beautiful night!
Without long delay,
Love each other right ✿

Imagine –

Ardor...

For orphans, she left 2 give charity.
The gift she gave provides great clarity.
They didn't resist
While closing their fist
& now they have what is a rarity 🐦

Imagine –

Graceful Attack...

Fire in hearts rage.
Soldiers await an order
2 flow like water.

Released from a cage,
They swim along the border
Just like an otter 🐾

Veils & Tales (pt. 1)…

As I place my eyes upon your nice breast,
Thoughts start 2 evaporate from the rest.
The beauty of melons is no contest
& my words become clumsily expressed.

I can not escape mentioning your grace
& style & your class written on your face.
It seems that nature competes in a race
2 flirt with your skin as it shows thru lace.

The verve felt in your presence will amaze.
Murmurs begin if one can't have a gaze.
Until your return, I wait in a daze
& remain impacted because u craze!

Imagine –

The Lion & Mermaid...

Deep within the huge Sahara Desert,
Walked a lion with a majestic mane.
He commands respect without much effort,
Well-knowing his ability 2 bane.
The awesome sun shines on his golden coat.
He preserves his fearless roar in his throat.

Lizards seem 2 wonder how it would be
2 move so proudly without a missed step:
"My green scaly skin for yours, I could see"
One says whilst starting a usual prep.
Close 2 the hot red sand, the light's shone
& within a blink, the lizard was gone.

There's a chance that it saw the huge eagle
Soar above danger 2 find a small meal.

Clear skies help the bird honor how regal
This gorgeous lion can handily kill.
Another brown eagle joins the blue space
& flies overhead as if in a race.

They fly with rigor & glide loftily.
One notices a faint movement below.
With sweeping advancements, both act softly
& in a flash, swap with assault & blow.
Life in their desert is a spectacle.
For continuance, orts are edible.

The gentle flies soon arrive in numbers.
They leave no chance for a moment to spare,
For they are also excellent hunters
Seizing openings left by those who dare.
Swarms investigate a possible dine
But dismally depart, forming a line.

Such as a king, the lion overlooks.
Small business does not warrant attention.

Screened from heat, he sits daintily in nooks.
Thereon, he stood 2 stun a convention.
He promenades akin 2 an artist,
Caresses the fans like a guitarist.

Before the caucus, some patrons harangue
Including a camel who views her post.
With voluble rampart, bereft of slang,
She critically acclaims our stately host!
Moved by her influence, the crowd becomes.
The excited monkeys beating on drums

Secure a rhythm the public wanted.
This welcoming atmosphere opens doors.
Before entering, for him, they daunted
Now, some on two feet whilst others on fours
Cheer for a doyen capable 2 lead.
Without questioning his reign, they accede.

Gross elephants station at the threshold,
Mighty & fearless & they honor him.

2 balk his prestige is sanction tenfold
So all in attendance fuse in a hymn.
Underwater (beneath their feet) she swims.
Unusual beauty betook her limbs

But perfect 2 the eyes if one looks on.
She belongs 2 her own queendom of sorts.
Unlike the lion with vigor & brawn,
The prominent mermaid orders her courts.
Using intuition opposed 2 whim,
She ploys atop an oasis 2 skim.

As if the sunbeams said take what u want,
She gathers radiation from that place.
Prey comes 2 her so she won't become gaunt.
Such is their affection towards Her Grace!
Highly draped in the best natural pearls,
Her favorite hairstyles consist of curls.

As the falling sun glistens on her tail,
Sparkles reflected on the lion's eye.

Unique 2 his nose, her fragrances sail
& now he feels what he dare not deny
Which is love for what he has not beheld.
He exits the meeting almost derailed.

On his way 2 possible ecstasy,
When stopped by a hyena who had words:
" O king! Dost thou require aught from me,
For I noticed a strange eye from my Lord's? "
But silent was His Crown, fixed on leaving
2 chase a notion somewhat deceiving.

Underwater she dove & quickly swam.
Far from the kingdom was this oasis.
Hyena went 2 tell a noble ram,
Worried for Lion who held this basis.
Confused as he walked due 2 her absence,
He looked like a tale told in the past tense.

Turning around 2 go back 2 his pride,
A bald vulture informs him of a mess.

Not knowing if he was 2 meet his bride,
The valiant lion ran fast 2 address
But on the way back, she wanted more sun.
Feeling her motion, it startled his run!

Left by the bald vulture leading the way,
Lion started a slow walk, well dismayed.
Not knowing if he'd ever see a day
That this strange attraction won't be delayed.
Apt 2 be responsible, he walks on
(Such is he who cares for even a pawn).

Arriving at his pride 2 view others,
Murmurs began without justified truth.
Uncertainty shown by the king smothers
Which amplifies voices even from youth.
One clever snake mounted a large boulder
& dangled above the lion's shoulder.

Speaking in his ear 2 ask a question
While onlookers wait 2 hear a reply,

The snake seemed 2 ignite a combustion.
Lion roared loudly causing birds 2 fly!
Vibrations ricocheted, piercing the sand,
Going beneath 2 a city so grand.

Ripples were interpreted by a carp
Who carried a word 2 a school of squid.
They relayed notes as if playing a harp
2 beast subaqueous swimming amid.
Reverberating melodies engulf.
Loyalty stops them from trying 2 bluff.

Some are mirthfully hoping 2 bear news
So they began moving along in sync.
At times, coral fish would playfully ruse,
Hid in reefs with an adorable wink.
Magical hues are everywhere one looks
Including amphibians found near brooks.

Glares from the setting sun relax their mood
So slowly they began swimming for her.

Traveling 2 her throne, some stopped for food.
The distance she covers is like a blur.
Greens turn dark blue the deeper they travel.
Some lose sight & begin 2 unravel.

Staying back due 2 fatigue & darkness,
Potential messengers retreat slowly.
Wishing they could express this with starkness,
Beautiful kinds leave while feeling lowly.
This wonderful mermaid glides gracefully.
Her style ensures that she judge tastefully.

Her intuition expects an account.
She seems 2 know wisdoms not often seen.
Aware before told about an amount,
She prepares 2 act prior 2 the scene.
She is glamorous with fairies' support!
Glitter brings about a small nymph's report:

" Above the ceiling, cries someone who yearns.
A suspected soul-mate, he just might be (♌/H).

Vibrations in the water somehow burns
With passion much unknown 2 land & sea. "
A full moon lit up the lion's kingdom
It's also loved by those in her queendom.

It seems that fairies show in bright moonlight.
Faithful 2 our mermaid, they bring good news.
One was known as the most beautiful sprite,
Carrying scrolls it would rather recuse.
Deep underwater, they converse in peace
& overhead, weather became caprice.

A long awaited rain cloud sneaks in view.
Scarab beetles move along quietly.
Midnight approaches. The sky turns dark blue
& owls float as far as the eye can see!
A mood of love surrounds this oasis.
Both of them want 2 explore new spaces.

The lion & mermaid began a thought.
They think about what brought all this 2 be.

Lion remembers what his mother taught
& Mermaid recalls her grandfather's glee.
Both would like a similar love affair
But they're not sure if the other would care.

Clouds begin 2 gather almost at once
As if they felt the same way as the two..
An event like this was seen as a bunce
Because prosperity seemed overdue.
Massive clouds ram into one another!
All over the dark blue sky, they smother.

Soft drops initially evaporate
But usher in nice sized drops that deluge.
Passionate rain begins 2 saturate
Sultry sand never looking for refuge.
Hidden creatures appear & bathe outside.
Lion sets out again 2 leave his pride.

Before he departs, he starts 2 ponder:
" How unfamiliar was that pheromone! "

Curious for answers 2 his wonder,
He starts 2 walk in the raindrops alone.
Beneath the sand (underwater) she glows
Many beautiful colors that she shows.

Asleep are the creatures in Lion's pride
But not owls & other nocturnal life
Yet, when they see His Majesty, they hide.
They want no parts in unwarranted strife.
Step after step, he continues a trail.
His heart remembers when his nostrils fail.

He walks down his high overlooking stage
In a direction he estimated.
Due 2 blinding rain that starts 2 enrage
His powerful mind so much, he waited.
Pouring rain plows into his soaking coat.
He starts 2 get cold & sees fairies float..

New 2 his eyes, but they are astounding!
Mesmerized, he begins 2 follow lead.

Suddenly, he forgets rain is pounding.
Glamour released by them make him concede!
Trailing behind glowing friends of a queen,
It feels like a dream he has never seen.

But onward he moves at a rhythmic pace.
The harder rain falls, the brighter they blush..
A humble, royal look rests on his face.
Darkness & rain bring about a soft hush.
Vivid lightning shows a long way 2 go
While she swims safely underwater slow.

The beautiful mermaid can feel power.
Lightning dances its way into water.
Thunder sounds loud & produce a shower.
Remembering words of her grandfather:
" Darling, your grandmother & I love u..
If she were here, she would tell u it's true.. "

Swimming pass a decorated mirror
(Looking at herself), not happy at all..

Tears mix in water. Nobody hears her
Crying 2 herself, wrapped up in a ball.
Her low self-esteem often makes her cry.
She wants it veiled so all her friends comply.

Thinking of her parents & why they left,
She begins 2 wonder about their care.
She feels that her beauty suffers from theft
Because her mom & dad were never there.
Given 2 her grandparents at her birth
Brings about questions regarding her worth.

She uncurls from her secured position
& with a deep sigh, swims out of the room.
Still able 2 hide her real condition,
She combs her long hair & picks up a broom.
As she sweeps her large pearls into a pile,
Past thoughts converge into another file.

Lost in the pearls, tears begin 2 subside
(She also loves many other crystals).

If one needs jewelry, she's well supplied.
She effects water in flower pistils.
She helps flowers grow devoid of the sun
By capturing rays with stones like no one.

Deep underwater, flowers make her smile.
She wants 2 forget struggles in her heart.
Now she's ready 2 model for a while.
She has an appreciation for art.
Swimming from one closet 2 another,
She knows not of a sister or brother.

Rich grandparents left her with their treasure
Before they disappeared in the tunnel.
She wears jewelry without care for measure
& well-knows that crystals help thoughts funnel.
Lady angler-fish seek her 2 commune.
They manage water weight, for they're immune.

Feeling this desire, Mermaid swims out.
She enters her courtyard awaiting them.

Little bright lights began shining about.
They also arrived 2 tell her of him.
A warm conversation began 2 spark.
They also would like what may be a lark.

They would like a region where all will be
Filled with happiness & have peace of mind.
Communities want 2 love being free
& have a place stocked with those who are kind.
These visions persist as many want more
& they are seen when she starts 2 explore.

Although she usually perceives well,
Her trusted friends have her full attention.
Within this fresh insight they came 2 tell,
Honesty moves what they have 2 mention.
Lion is still mesmerized by fairies
Who aren't conditioned by who one marries!

Passing bones of animals slain before,
He continues each step with extreme trust.

Not knowing his love is at a seafloor,
His pride inside make him have 2 adjust!
Consistent motion in darkness & rain
Makes a rhythm he feels can ease her pain.

Sometimes, love makes one feel like a genius.
Stars are much more luminous in the night.
We rarely consider what's under us.
It's here all the time but out of our sight.
This world has levels many never see,
For they're too tangled on one 2 break free.

Many wait 2 be told how 2 have fun.
They remain isolated & afraid.
Secretly watching others in the sun,
Only wishing 2 join life's big parade.
Negative thoughts consume what u let it.
Stay positive as long as stars are lit.

Nothing should prevent one from seeking love.
It brings wisdom & balance when truthful.

Praise increase while blessings come from above.
Time may lapse but these hearts still feel youthful.
Mermaid prepares herself 2 be honored.
Changing stones & suddenly, she pondered.

Her deep thoughts swim as well as her body.
She worries about how he may appear:
" Does he collect stones like me for hobby
Or make believe happiness conquers fear? "
So many questions make way for discounts.
Starting 2 feel uncertain, she miscounts!

Frustrations set in & then come despair.
After all, beauty in him may not shine..
Broken hearts may not believe love is fair.
Evil pretends 2 be love 2 confine.
Shown how a male looks when he loves his wife,
She will accept nothing less for her life!

Courageous emotions creep in her heart:
" If he can't see my point of views, he's wrong..

I was not looking for him from the start
So he'd better not wish 2 stay here long.."
Angry without a cause & now she sings
(An ancient tune she chose for what it brings)

Melodies that unite all those who feel.
Even cold blooded ones enjoy the sound.
Able 2 make imaginations real,
These magical words she sing are profound!
The pouring rain stops immediately.
Lion walks a road now easy 2 see.

He soaks with eyes fixed on the little ones
Who start quietly vanishing from sight.
The way they captivate with glamour stuns.
He sees them disappear into the night.
A cloudy, dark night prevents a gallop.
He's shocked when he kicks shells of a scallop!

Thirsty & almost out of energy,
Lion bows for a drink of rainwater.

Not knowing he was led by synergy,
Lion's face submerged when he felt hotter.
Surprised 2 hear sounds, he opens his eyes!
Glowing fairies never said their goodbyes..

Breathless, he quickly snatches his head out
(Wiping his eyes & gathering himself).
His huge paws now slowly cover his snout,
For this is not what gets put on the shelf!
Lion senses this is not just by chance.
His brave nature pushes him 2 advance.

He looks around but the darkness is thick.
He drinks more water with his eyes open
Awaiting lights after every lick.
He's unaware of this branch of ocean
But quenched, he brought his head out once again.
The absent sprites make his walk seem in vain.

Exhausted by the efforts, he lays flat
(Breathing heavily as emotions bleed).

A frog leaps trying 2 escape a bat
& that made our huge clever cat take heed!
Quick 2 his feet, he watched the frog survive
By jumping in the pool 2 stay alive!

Lion then noticed the depth & volume,
For it's not simply a puddle of rain.
Mermaid's now decorating her ballroom,
Singing & forgetting about her pain.
Lion stoops & moves cautiously once more.
Staring at his reflection, his heart tore.

Disappointed when he didn't see lights,
He dips his head & leaves his eyes ajar.
Suddenly, the escorts come back in sight!
They show a map 2 a city afar.
Overwhelmed by glee, Lion dives inside!
Scared fish warn that a danger may betide.

Our huge royal cat never swam before
& water was always a fear of his!

Little ones showed him what may be in store.
He then tried 2 relieve himself of this.
Retreating, he pulls out with his forearm
& shakes water off 2 not bring more harm..

END OF PART ONE

The Lion & Mermaid

Meditation, Strength & Rubies...

Shine bright with the sun & glow with the moon.
Take care like the wind when the breeze is soft.
Sit securely above rooms as a loft
& float comfortably like a balloon.
This era is different than before.
The ocean seems 2 be further from shore.

Don't allow what eludes 2 harm your soul.
Keep your heart clean & think well of the good.
Lessons were taught by those who understood
& they left drafts on how 2 reach your goal.
Take heed 2 these words & apply with thought.
U may see benefits that can't be bought.

Today is anew so give yourself hope.
Yesterday is gone & u are still here.
Some whispers help when they approach your ear
So cheer yourself & don't give in 2 mope.
Sometimes, communication helps others.
Your welfare's vital just as another's 🐛

Mirror Love...

How many ways does openings occur?
Women & gentlemen work together.
Happiness seems 2 extend one's tether
Even with little help from the weather.
Memories improve from how things once were.

Insight enables mirrors 2 bring joy.
Will u love yourself for once in your life?
Thoughts of self-hatred may cut like a knife
& cause unwarranted feelings of strife
Instead of those u should really employ.

Please don't allow your peers 2 deceive u!
Sometimes, they are just influenced themselves.
They put what's beneficial on the shelves
& masquerade as if they're evil elves
Perhaps 2 steal what u know 2 be true 🍎

Don't Forget Your Receipt...

It may be easy 2 see faults in others
But when it comes 2 our own, we are blind.
One may have tried 2 touch a thousand lovers
Only 2 see that love is not hard 2 find.

One may travel the world 2 find a jewel
& crystals & fossils of precious types
Forgetting 2 honor their innate tool,
The one that pressure didn't burst the pipes.

2 look within yourself takes a lot of care.
You'll need courage & other attributes.
Accepting much better for yourself is rare.
Just look around & see all the acts of brutes.

Giants & Politics...

Precious blessings enter hearts,
Those in honorary states.
An empty promise imparts
Insignias tasting of tarts,
Allowing 2 see from starts
How far lemons are from dates.
Some with efforts try 2 trick
Many who may not be wise.
Those who build their home of brick
Surely can absorb a stick
Striking it lick after lick
But only grow from the tries 🍎

Colors & Fabrics...

Questions of size are no longer needed.
The rules of engagement are set in stone.
Unnatural fashions are succeeded
By realizations when we're alone,
Accepting images when they are shown.
This severe process may help 2 atone.

Mature behavior & classy command
Display stunning style, brimming zestfully!
The infectious influence is so grand,
For it will impact those addressed fully.
Elegant secrets are confessed fully
Thru blank talks that make us impressed fully.

At this stage, we see colors & fabrics.
Imported feathers, some nice 2 the touch,
Work well for comfort while plying tactics.
Suppressed egos & vanities & such
Help one 2 avoid the enemy's clutch
& successfully frees us from his hutch 🌹

For My Beloved Sisters & Brothers...

O Allah! Please protect the Muslim.
Please make us united & built 2 last.
Mecca, Medina & Jerusalem
Are targeted by nations of the past.

Give us the tools we need 2 stop this war!
Don't let these bandits humiliate love.
Make examples out of them like before
Because they're monsters who carelessly shove.

Grant us victory & patience 2 grow.
Guide us 2 that which is better 2 do.
Bless us 2 teach what all of them should know
& raise the ranks of those who walk us thru
(Amen).

We May Be Better Off...

Life may have seemed 2 be much more simpler.
Nowadays, people complicate the land
As if they have thoughts of an emperor,
Dictating lifestyles for the upper hand.

If a person was proud 2 be God's slave
& go about works in obedience,
Never once calculating what he gave
Or just take routes for convenience,

He may be better off ❀

Mysterious Bird...

They're hungry for substance,
Held together with hope.
Enemies will advance
If gifts get out of scope.

Needs are useful at once.
Birds hardly ever store
So everyday one stunts
Believing it will score.

Relying on The God,
They trust again today.
Some may think it looks odd
When they wash dirt away.

They receive everyday
& sleep content at night.
Up at the first sun ray,
Trying with all their might.

Efforts until they die
Are shown with naught 2 waste.
Love for the next 2 fly
Ensures they're not effaced.

May we learn & go tell
The lessons that u show?
They help u 2 sleep well.
Together we can grow 🐾

Bathe in Beads...

Remember how fortunate we may be.
Wind blows easily by The Will of God.
Take into account the two types of sea
& how air we breathe is cleansed by the tree.
Beauty in nature can be seen abroad.

Remember how fortunate u may be.
Perhaps an incomparable abode
Is prepared for u so favorably
& showers of happiness unworldly
May be there for u although you're not owed.

Bathe in beads that remind u of fortune
(Beads that remind u 2 seek forgiveness).
Buy from merchants & be back for more soon
Because u may notice just before noon
One can't live longer than due nor live less ✿

Elite Lovers...

O u elite lovers!
Ask Allah 2 help us.
Your roots are infectious.
U teach what uncovers.

O u elite circle!
Words like yours are so sweet,
Rich, & such a good treat.
Your heart's more than purple.

O u elite lovers!

O our elite sages!
Hearts open as u shine.
Your traces build a shrine
Sometimes, seen for ages.

Elite ones who love God,
How precious are your palms!
Your fragrance is as alms
Found in dreams that are odd.

O u elite lovers!

Perfume & Poetry...

As I pour water into your bathtub,
I see the lights change from purple 2 green.
Blue crystals are used for a body rub
As u rest in water feeling serene.
Heat under the bubbles rise 2 the air
Where fragrance from candles welcomes it there.

Heartbeats are rhythms for music & such.
Dance in the spirit around in a daze.
We join together with every touch
2 help bring our thoughts from out of a maze.
Beautiful energy surrounds the mood
As I become lost & stiff where I stood.

U caress my love & tease my body
& I explore your delicious nature.
Fly thru castles & laugh in the lobby.
I will continue & join u later.
We are safe & outwitting enemies
Who'd love 2 see strife atop miseries.

Honesty motivates passion & joy.
The mirrors show gratitude bold & sweet.
U make me move as if I were a toy.
Our welcomed sloppiness bereft of neat
Overcomes our fancies we feel inside
& washes on shore like a raging tide!

Mountains may crumble when the giants come
Walking as if drunk & clumsy for rest.
Sleep well for now u most beautiful bum
She utters before snoozing on my chest.
The sunbeams awaken the little birds
Hungry for happiness & nice soft words 🐦

Yellow Jasmines...

Picture a field of beautiful yellow flowers in your mind.
Imagine u & I in the midst & very hard 2 find

Laughing & playing with tranquility in our soul
As we escape the mean world for our own control 🌼

The Farmer, Baker & Server...

How easily does dirt set on a garb?
Imagine: Farmer, Baker & Server.
She severs fruit with what's sharp as a barb
& handles the apples with sweet fervor.
Her precious hands carefully touch his heart
Thru selecting fruit like a work of art.

He masters the heat so effortlessly.
Experience moved on him as a youth.
Customers know he will insert freshly
Chopped apples sweet enough 2 rot a tooth.
People return due 2 service & taste.
They leave satisfied with no food 2 waste.

Alone in his shop, the baker believes
His married supplier may sneak away.
Looking at golden fruit, his mind conceives
A plan 2 invite her over today.
The unseen server helps him with his plan.
It knows many tricks 2 teach this poor man.

Her neat apple farm is around a lake
With green grass cultivated by her spouse.
She goes 2 pluck but startled by a snake
On its way 2 smother a little mouse.
Just as she paused, a thought enters her mind
2 kiss her husband for being so kind

But he is away on another trip
& the unseen server whispers 2 her.
She rejects thoughts but one, she didn't skip,
For this day, love guided them 2 enter.
Angry & wanting 2 just get some air,
She strolls 2 the baker not far from there.

Bells situated notifies Baker
That someone walked inside 2 be honored.
Seeing her glare, he wanted 2 take her
Places in his mind he often pondered.
She's not here for that. She wanted a pie.
She states her business with tears in her eye.

It's fresh from the kiln so it has 2 cool.
He tells her 2 wait while he cleans a seat.
Hoping she doesn't notice his mouth drool
While gathering what he needs for her treat,
He makes his way 2 her quiet table.
The unseen server makes him feel able

2 convince her that it's okay 2 weep
& touch her shoulder as he pours the milk.
The unseen server told him something deep
& then his language became smooth as silk.
She asked for her pie 2 make him depart,
For she knows how 2 keep dirt off her heart 🍎

Candle Wax...

The worlds are grand, encased with levels.
U can go thru many dimensions.
Beware of the beautiful devils.
They are easily provoked rebels,
Eager 2 bring u 2 pretensions.

Like candle wax used 2 light the gloom,
Your soul is the flame whilst your body's wax.
The more u melt, the brighter the room.
Walls around u begin 2 consume
Your passionate heat shining thru cracks.

Just as sunbeams pierce thru the graveyards
& crows & blackbirds fly overhead,
Symbols & signs are there on your cards
But death sneaks & strikes right thru your guards
& claims another who joins the dead!

Let's bring ourselves 2 where we can drop
(A cliff that shows universal views).
Let's fall. Never expecting 2 stop
Is what will take us straight 2 the top
& give us what we thought we would lose.

Can u hear your lonely, quiet voice
(The one abused when u were a child)?
Remember u thought u had no choice
But then u found that u can rejoice?
It made it all worth the pain you've piled ✸

Woozy Aquanaut...

Coffee & incense make a red hot dish.
Good love in the air makes a man not wish
Except for a touch that could move his soul
2 a place that is the ultimate goal.

Cracks in the wall add character inside.
Cigarette smoke blown by gangsters that smile
Makes sure one respects 2 not offend pride
While women walk courageously in style.

Movements are orchestrated by me
2 see that children live comfortably.
We could move together in honesty
& learn 2 be firm as roots on a tree.

Keeping up with antique wizard's magic
Brought her 2 those who know well its blueprint.
After shopping with currency too spent,
It strangled all what was seen but tragic.

Beautiful outlooks with ascetic rays
Nullify conjectures that bring u down.
Plans were revealed 2 honor night & days,
Not for showoff in unproductive ways
But 2 pull us from what causes 2 drown
By guiding thru this mystical maze 🐞

I Am Not Perfect...

I am not perfect.

Traces of my past
Keep me running fast
2 a place correct

But I'm not there yet.
This long way 2 go
For what I did sow
After the sunset

Shows when time rises.
I recall the grave.
The road that I pave
Reveals surprises

& I'm not perfect ❧

Lustful Thoughts...

Lustful thoughts fill the room as they mingle.
Her hair is in the way but he can feel.
Bodies shiver in delight & tingle
While they embrace the degrees like a seal ✿

Lavender World...

A lavender world is a world of love
Filled with good wishes & hopes we dream of.

The heart of the people is where they think.
They move about thru mixed purple & pink.

A lavender world is not of nonsense.
It's where lovely people become intense.

A Mission Never Done...

He never knew she already had a love.
She made sure that he did not know.
She was the one he always dreamed of
But her feelings for him will soon grow.

If she plays her cards & win the game,
She will have both men as one
But if she plays a queen instead of an ace,
Her mission will never be done.

Her mind is made up that she wants both men.
Her fantasy is 2 keep them both!
Her love for one grew stronger since then
& 2 him she makes an oath

That she won't play with his heart or tame his mind
Like an animal in the circus
But in doing that, her mission could never be done.

Why are locks not hard 2 find when keys are what u need?
Is love a feeling of sharing or is love a feeling of greed?

Should we ask the people in love
Or one who has been mistreated?
If they have not retreated,
Maybe they will know how 2 move ❧

Potent Essence...

She wasn't faithful.
He knew how she was.
Her heart was hateful.
He's ridiculous ✿

Used Like Glue...

I feel lonely because I can't have u.
My body is lost if u don't have time.
Without your love, I don't know what 2 do.
My words are in prose devoid of a rhyme.

Some nights, I wish u were lying right there.
Other nights, I wonder what I will do.
Sometimes, I think I would just sit & stare
But most likely, we'll become used like glue 🌸

Jewelry in Boxes...

I'm impatient when it comes 2 pleasure.
Your soulful touch is soft as a feather.
Pirates would travel 2 have your treasure
But I'll stand guard for u thru the weather ✸

Hush & Listen...

I didn't love u until it made me
Realize truth & what it forbade me.
I can't stop these feelings from coming.
I'm hooked on your sense & find it stunning!
I don't know what 2 do & friend's advice
Most assuredly add vice as I think twice.
When I am alone & thinking of u,
I hush & listen & know what 2 do.

Jihaad on My Heart...
(Written on behalf of a friend)

A clash of cultures emerged from illness.
One was unaware of the other's ways.
Heart attack brought about a price one pays
As he would lay on a bed in stillness.

Long ago, he would not have imagined
This relationship & he knew his plight.
His side was accused of acts causing fright.
It left many in his culture saddened.

Options dwindled because experts are rare.
The reputation of one resonates.
As his dreadful condition escalates,
Encouragement 2 see him came from care.

Family members investigate well.
Time doesn't allow blind judgement 2 speak
So all those who love the poor man would seek
Help as emotions are locked in a cell.

An operation would have 2 be made!
Usually, they won't allow his touch.
It doesn't hurt that his manners are such
Of a peaceful type that will surely aid.

Successful in every way they could look
Was a recovery that stuns many.
They've looked for traces but can't find any
& what's not a weapon's now a hand shook 🐛

Forest Signs...

We watched the rainfall.
Nobody uttered a word
2 keep secrets locked.

Within a short stall,
There came signals from a bird
That cleared what was blocked 🌸

I Come With An Egyptian Mau...

I sail the Milky Way with a great key.
Support from past masters gave it 2 me.

I touch the Nile with the nose of this boat
Before it coasts the waves 2 calmly float.

I have beside me an Egyptian Mau.
It outsmarts darkness if I don't know how.

Darkness can't see it but it sees the snake
Try 2 swallow light before I awake.

I welcome the light that's shone from the past,
The tranquil glow that shows what may contrast.

That powerful shine doesn't make one vain.
It rebirths those who want 2 live again.

The key unlocks doors hidden by the night.
Mau is victor when it & the snake fight.

It's also a gift from those of past days
For protection against a snake who preys.

The serpent comes 2 steal & swallow truth
But it's trumped by an Egyptian Mau's tooth

Protecting a key that unlocks the sky
& bring about that on which we rely.

I'm sure 2 come with an Egyptian Mau 🐾

THANK YOU!

81321997R00094

Made in the USA
Lexington, KY
15 February 2018